IE Survival Guide Standard III

Instructions
Orientation in Space II
Transitive Relations
Syllogisms
Representational Stencil Design

Dr. Lynn Brown

This book is dedicated to my family and friends who encouraged me to learn and push my own thinking so that I may have a significant impact on others.

It is also dedicated to my colleagues who believe in the malleability of the human brain and that thinking should be explicitly taught instead of just caught.

Copyright © 2012 by Frameworks, LLC. All rights reserved.
ISBN 978-0-9884091-2-5

Table of Contents

Overview..4

Instructions..6

Orientation in Space II..37

Transitive Relations..56

Syllogisms...81

Representational Stencil Design........................ 118

IE Survival Guide
Standard III
Overview

This booklet is an unauthorized guide and in no way supplants the Instrumental Enrichment Teacher's Guide. Instead it is intended to be a help to the classroom teacher during their first year of implementation. These are my observations and experiences from my first year of teaching IE with helpful input from a teacher colleague. Each instrument begins with an introduction of the overall goal(s) of the instrument, followed by possible ways to teach the cover page, then aids for teaching each page. The aids for specific pages are divided into three parts:

1. Things to Consider – important ideas/concepts on each page.
2. Work on the Sheet – some possible ways to introduce the page and discussions you may want to have as you work with students.
3. Closure - Discussion for Insight – possible topics you may want to cover. Remember this depends entirely on your class discussion and you may not even cover the suggestions stated here but your conversation may lead to something else.

Overall Goal of IE: Make the learner more changeable, open to learning, and self-regulated. They become AWARE and more in charge of their own learning.

Instrumental Enrichment is not just about getting the correct answers. You are teaching **cognitive behaviors** or thinking skills as found in the Process Standards of the Common Core State Standards (CCSS). These cognitive behaviors are aligned to the following sources in the CCSS:

English Language Arts
Qualities of Students Who Are College and Career Ready in Writing, Speaking and Listening
Mathematics
Characteristics of Mathematically Proficient Students

The student must be an active participant in this process of change. It is your job to increase the student's awareness of his or her own thinking so that they experience a deeper understanding, not just you. The big idea is NOT to finish the sheet or find the correct answers, (though finishing the sheet with correct answers helps crystalize concepts). Rather, it is to cause the student to change his or her own thinking through mediation (MLE). You must be very intentional in your responses/questioning to increase this awareness and empower the student. Catch them being brilliant or notice when they are doing something desired. For example, "I noticed you didn't erase that one. You made a plan before beginning which showed a restraint of impulsivity."

Remember, the ultimate goal is to empower the student to develop the ability to mediate themselves.

IE Survival Guide
Instructions

<u>Goal</u>
Instructions is about giving and receiving written instructions. Encoding and decoding verbal or graphic information.

<u>Big Ideas:</u>
- Precise and complete information is required of the giver to enable the receiver to interpret the meaning accurately.
- Explicit instructions have a greater chance of accurate interpretation compare to implicit instructions.
- In the presence of ambiguity one uses strategies to find the intended meaning.

There is so much potential for mediation on each page of this instrument. These are only suggestions. It is important to let what the students are doing and let your noticing drive the mediation. For example, if you plan to talk about precision but the students change strategies, notice the change in strategy and make the students aware of that. There will be plenty of opportunity to talk about precision on another page.

Cover Page

In my experience, I have found that you don't need to beat the individual pieces of the cover page to death. In other words don't spend so much time on each part that you lose students' interest. The following are potential discussions. Don't do them all at once since you will have 4 more opportunities (one for each instrument) to cover salient points.

Logo (a thinker) - simple, memorable, visual (you may have the student put their picture here)
Discuss "What does it mean to think?"
- Brainstorm: recalling, remembering, reflecting, making decisions, having ideas, solving problems, planning to do something, imagining, anticipating, and drawing conclusions.

Talk about problem solving. What is involved?
- Make a chart: get students to list: identify the problem, gather information (through our senses – give examples) consider possible courses of action/solutions, make a plan, carry out the plan, and check for accuracy.

Example: I use a hypothetical problem – I need to ride my bike but I can't: What's the problem? Is it the tire? The chain?

Title – *Instructions*

Symbol - Ask the students what they notice. Invite them to hypothesize the meaning of the symbol. They probably notice a lot of information and several paths that can be followed to and from the result.

Slogan - "Just a Moment . . . LET ME THINK!" This stays the same throughout all the Standard Instruments. It conveys an idea of calmness of the mind. We have time to think and thinking takes time. Some answers take more time to think about than others. It is normal/necessary to think before completing a task.
In *Mind Set* Carol Dweck says that people with fixed mind sets believe smart people already know and therefore don't need time to

think. However, a person who has a growth mind set believes learning is a process which takes time and effort. This also helps with restraining impulsivity. Encourage students to think before they act/ answer.

Page 1

Things to Consider
Pages 1 – 4 develop the language and concepts to do the rest of the instrument.
Concepts being developed on this page include:
- Labeling
- Clear perception
- Precision/accuracy
- Visual transport

Work on the Sheet
Students complete the sheet.

Look at column one and use labels and vocabulary to describe what is being seen. Use visual transport to duplicate the model in from the first column in the second column. The third column already contains the word (although the extra lines suggest more is expected). You may want the students to add to the words in column 3. For example, add the word "diagonal" to the first example.

Closure - Discussion for Insight
Discuss the implicit meaning of the one word directions: look, draw, and write.

Universal labels help communicate unchanging characteristics of a figure.

The final step in following directions is to check for accuracy.

Page 2

Things to Consider
Pages 1 – 4 develop the language and concepts to do the rest of the instrument.
Concepts being developed on this page include:
- Labeling
- Clear perception
- Precision/accuracy
- Visual transport

Work on the Sheet
Students complete the sheet.
Notice the scaffolding in column 3: the first two are done for the student, the third and fourth ones are partially complete (the student needs to add "rectangle" to the existing "orange," and "black" to "circle") the last one requires the whole answer from the student.

Closure - Discussion for Insight
Using existing cues to complete a task. The one word direction "write" is ambiguous – how much description is required? The cues (examples) show the acceptable parameters: color and shape are sufficient.

Page 3

Things to Consider
Pages 1 – 4 develop the language and concepts to do the rest of the instrument.
Concepts being developed on this page include:
- Labeling
- Clear perception
- Precision/accuracy
- Visual transport

Work on the Sheet
Students complete the sheet.
Complexity increases throughout this page.
#4 switches from telling to describing – there is a difference.

Closure - Discussion for Insight
It is helpful to read all directions before beginning. In example 2, if you read the first seven words and carried them out, you might have a different result than what is generated after reading the whole statement.
When an object has no right or left – such as a square or circle – we impose the direction from our point of view. (tie in from *Orientation in Space I*)

Page 4

Things to Consider
Pages 1 – 4 develop the language and concepts to do the rest of the instrument.
Concepts being developed on this page include:
- Labeling
- Clear perception
- Precision/accuracy
- Visual transport

Work on the Sheet
Students complete the sheet.
This page introduces the imaginary division of the frame into halves or quarters (which increases precision).

In number two there are many ways to draw the squares.

Closure - Discussion for Insight
Possibilities for discussion:
In some directions, sequence is important and in some it doesn't matter. How do we know when it matters?
Discuss ambiguity in directions, for example in number two. There may be more than one possible answer or additional information might need to be given if the intent was for one solution.

Implicit information - the size of the figures will not be the same in all solutions. Some may draw them larger or smaller but there is a range of acceptable solutions.

Page 5

Things to Consider
This page introduces a higher level of precision through the use of the word between and dividing the frame into nine imaginary areas much like a tic-tac-toe diagram using top, middle, bottom, left, center, and right.

Work on the Sheet
Students complete the sheet.

Closure - Discussion for Insight
In case of ambiguous directions, select the most plausible solution. Sometimes there is a difference in the intended message and the strict meaning of a phrase (denotation/connotation). For example in number four, draw a line. A line is straight but you can't complete the task with a straight line. The connotation of line and intent of the directions allows it to be curved.

A framework (tic-tac-toe diagram) helps organize. Bridge this to the school framework. This shows expectations and dictates behavior according to its norms. Other frameworks may include family, church, Boy or Girl Scouts, or athletic teams.

Page 6

Things to Consider
This page is summative for pages 1 – 5.
This page can get long and tedious for some students. It may take so long for them to finish it that you have little time left for discussion. You may want to cut the examples into strips and have each student complete one strip.

Work on the Sheet
Students complete the sheet or 1 task.

Closure - Discussion for Insight
Discussion - how much precision is required? Notice how much space is given to complete the task. This implies a need for precision in language used. Do not allow students to use another piece of paper to write volumes to describe each task. The challenge is to be concise.

Page 7

Things to Consider
Pages 7 and 8 introduce the ideas of having a starting point and using the edges of the frame as reference points.

Work on the Sheet
Students complete the sheet.

Closure - Discussion for Insight
The same result can be achieved from a number of different starting points.
Emphasize the importance of using precise language.

Page 8

Things to Consider
More practice with having a starting point and using the edges of the frame as reference points.

Work on the Sheet
Students complete the sheet.

Closure - Discussion for Insight
Directions given in the form of a list can be easier to follow and easier to check.
Some tasks must be carried out in a defined sequence in order to achieve the desired result.

Page 9

Things to Consider
This page sums up pages 7 and 8 and provides opportunity for error analysis.

Work on the Sheet
Students complete the sheet.

Closure - Discussion for Insight
Precision and less ambiguity. A statement can be true but not precise. It might be good for describing but not for instructing. When does it matter and when doesn't it matter?

Page 10

Things to Consider
Provides practice in ordering according to size while following written directions.

Work on the Sheet
Students complete the sheet.

Closure - Discussion for Insight
Discuss strategies:
- Read through all directions before beginning.
- Where did you start?
- Integrating instructions and checking for error.

Page 11

Things to Consider
It is possible to express the same idea in a number of ways.

Work on the Sheet
Students complete the sheet.

Closure - Discussion for Insight
Compare the directions in #1 to the directions in #6. Using size order is a concise way of describing relationships.

Ordering unlike shapes by size is more ambiguous. A taller triangle may have less area than a shorter square, but we often use height of an unlike figure to rank size.

Page 12

Things to Consider
Decode more complex directions.

Work on the Sheet
Students complete the sheet.

Closure - Discussion for Insight
When directions are complex and unorganized we must read carefully and reorganize the information in order to complete the task successfully.

Negative directions tell us what not to do but do not tell us what to do. The can be helpful in eliminating possibilities (ambiguity). Checking finished work is important to ensure correctness or accuracy.

Page 13

Things to Consider
Practice describing the contents of the frames in the most economical way (precise language).

Creativity - find freedom within the constraints.

Work on the Sheet
Students are limited to the three lines given. Additional space is not allowed.

Since there are five examples, you could also do some of them verbally focusing on precise language with no repeating allowed.

Closure - Discussion for Insight
Discuss how students decided what was most relevant.

Example of giving directions to my home - I don't need to describe every house and building you will pass but I might mention an important landmark, for example next to a big, red barn.

Page 14

Things to Consider
Pages 14 and 15 are error correction pages with emphasis on size order.

Work on the Sheet
Students complete the sheet.

Closure - Discussion for Insight
There are two sources of error:
1. The written directions were not precise and complete
2. The written directions were not followed accurately

Page 15

Things to Consider
Pages 14 and 15 are error correction pages with emphasis on size order.

Work on the Sheet
Students complete the sheet.

Closure - Discussion for Insight
There are two sources of error:
1. The written directions were not precise and complete
2. The written directions were not followed accurately

Pages 16 and 17

Things to Consider
Pages 16 and 17 focus on the concepts of vertical, horizontal and diagonal. If students are proficient in these concepts, you may want to skip these pages.

Work on the Sheet
Students complete the sheet.

Closure - Discussion for Insight
The concept horizontal means parallel to the horizon. Vertical refers to a line being perpendicular to the horizon. Diagonals are mathematical concepts related to a figure, not the horizon. A diagonal connects two nonadjacent corners of a geometric figure. A diagonal may appear to be horizontal or vertical depending on the orientation of the figure it lies within.

Page 18

Things to Consider
Review the concepts of horizontal, vertical, and diagonal lines.
Work systematically to complete complex tasks.

Work on the Sheet
Students complete the sheet.

Closure - Discussion for Insight
There is a difference between what we see and what we know – or there is a difference in how three dimensional figures are represented on a two dimensional piece of paper.
How did students count the lines of the windmill? On each side of the windmill we see three line segments. Yet we know that each side is composed of just one line.

How did students mark the lines? Did they go over the page three times: once for vertical lines, again for horizontal lines, and again for diagonal lines? Did they mark all the lines first and go back to count them or did they count as they marked? Discuss the pros and cons of each method.

Page 19

Things to Consider
This is an AV page that provides an opportunity to practice and reinforce previous learning. Depending on the needs of your students you may choose to do it or skip it.

Work on the Sheet
Students complete the sheet.

Closure - Discussion for Insight
Possible discussion point - this page is rather complex yet students are able to complete it. Why? Familiarity with a task increases efficiency. Practice makes perfect.

Page 20

Things to Consider
Practice with precise description.

This page can take a long time for students to compete. You may want to assign two examples for students to write, share those, and then challenge students to do the other examples verbally.

Work on the Sheet
Students complete the sheet.

Closure - Discussion for Insight
Discuss successes and failures. What were causes of failures and reasons for successes?

Page 21

Things to Consider
Focus on planning behavior – not reading all the directions first may lead to errors or the inability to complete the task.

Work on the Sheet
Students complete the sheet.

Closure - Discussion for Insight
Complex tasks must be planned before starting. Give examples from life - starting to mix cookie batter before realizing you don't have enough of one ingredient or starting a homework assignment and finding you don't have a required colored pencil (or other material).

Page 22

Things to Consider
Use a coded figure to improve precision and avoid wordiness.

Work on the Sheet
Students complete the sheet.

Closure - Discussion for Insight
Codes can work well but all communicating parties must understand the code. "Side one of a triangle" is not helpful unless I know which side is side one.
The code stays constant even when the figure changes orientation.

Pages 23 and 24

Things to Consider
These are review pages which require the student to apply the concepts and strategies learned so far in the unit. They are very similar in look and task to pages 14 and 15 but include more concepts and vocabulary.

Work on the Sheet
Students complete the sheets.

Closure - Discussion for Insight
When things are very similar we must be especially careful to distinguish between them (the last column changes from draw to write).

Ask students to discuss interesting changes. #7 requires a small change (just a change in one digit: no. 2 to no. 1) but makes a big difference in the figure.

Page 25

Things to Consider
Describe a figure precisely and completely.

Reproduce a figure from a written description.

Work on the Sheet
You may want to assign two of the examples to each student.

Closure - Discussion for Insight
Discuss: clear, adequate, and true.

Page 26

Things to Consider
This page is similar to page 18 but requires finding parallel lines.

Work on the Sheet
Students complete the sheet.

Closure - Discussion for Insight
Discussion can also be similar to discussion from page 18:
There is a difference between what we see and what we know – or there is a difference in how three dimensional figures are represented on a two dimensional piece of paper. The back horizontal line of the suitcase is one line conceptually but three line segments optically.

What strategies did students use? Discuss the pros and cons of each method.

Page 27

Things to Consider
Distinguish between nested figures and intersecting figures.

Work on the Sheet
Students complete the sheet.

Closure - Discussion for Insight
Careful planning is necessary in order to have a center that is common to two or more figures.

Page 28

Things to Consider
Show mastery of the instrument.

Work on the Sheet
This is another page where the time it takes to finish all the writing may leave little or no time to discuss. Break up the task by having students complete 1 or 2 tasks in written for and another 1 or 2 verbally or cut the sheets apart and give one example to each student.

Closure - Discussion for Insight
Summarize the instrument by having the students create a mind map.

Page 29

Things to Consider
Pages 29 and 30 introduce a third dimension. On this page the students are constructing the figures, on page 30 they are describing the figures.
The definitions of terms changes from 2 dimensions to 3 dimensions. For example, above, below, on top of, and under.

Work on the Sheet
Students complete the sheet.

Closure - Discussion for Insight
What is below is covered by what is above therefore it may be necessary to start with the uppermost figure when drawing (working backwards).

Page 30

Things to Consider
Describe three dimensional figures.
The definitions of terms changes from 2 dimensions to 3 dimensions. For example, above, below, on top of, and under.

Work on the Sheet
This is another page where the time it takes to finish all the writing and may leave little or no time for discussion. Break up the task by having students complete 1 or 2 tasks in written for and another 1 or 2 verbally or cut the sheets apart and give one example to each student.

Closure - Discussion for Insight
Possible discussion points:
- Which was easier, page 29 or 30? Why?
- Task 1 is the bottom figure a square or a rectangle? Does it matter?

IE Survival Guide
Orientation in Space II

Goal
Orientation in Space II is about spatial orientation, its representation, and communication in a universal instead of personal system.

Big Ideas:
- Introduces external, stable, absolute systems of reference.
- Reduction of egocentrism - realize there are different viewpoints. We can put ourselves in the place of another person to see a situation from his or her viewpoint.

There is so much potential for mediation on each page of this instrument. What follows are only suggestions. It is important to allow the students' to do their work and to let your observations drive the mediation. For example, if you plan to talk about precision but the students change strategies, notice the change in strategy and make the students aware of that change in strategy. There will be plenty of opportunity to talk about precision on another page.

Cover Page

In my experience, I have realized that I don't need to endlessly repeat the individual pieces of the cover page. In other words, don't spend so much time on each part that you lose students' interest. The following are constructs and ideas for potential discussions. Don't do them all at once since you will have three more opportunities (one for each instrument) to cover the salient points.

Logo (a thinker) - simple, memorable, visual (you may have the student put their picture here)
Discuss "What does it mean to think?"
- Brainstorm: recalling, remembering, reflecting, making decisions, having ideas, solving problems, planning to do something, imagining, anticipating, and drawing conclusions.

Talk about problem solving. What is involved?
- Make a chart: get students to list: identify the problem, gather information – (through our senses – give examples) consider possible courses of action/solutions, make a plan, carry out the plan, and check for accuracy.

Example: I use a hypothetical problem – I need to ride my bike but I can't: What's the problem? Is it the tire? The chain?

Title – *Orientation in Space II*

Symbol - Ask the students what they notice. Invite them to hypothesize the meaning of the symbol: a compass to orient us or compass rose to identify directions on a map. This is yet another way we organize our world e.g. with cardinal directions or lines of latitude and longitude.

Slogan - "Just a Moment . . . LET ME THINK!" This remains the same throughout all the Standard Instruments. It conveys an idea of calmness of the mind. We have time to think and thinking takes time. Some answers take more time to think through than others. It is normal/necessary to think before completing a task.

In *Mind Set* Carol Dweck says that people with fixed mind sets believe smart people already know and therefore don't need time to think. However, a person who has a growth mind set believes learning is a process which takes time and effort. This also helps with restraining impulsivity. Encourage students to think before they act/answer.

Page 1

Things to Consider
- Review the idea of a closed system.
- Internalize the relationship of north, south, east, and west to each other.

Work on the Sheet
Students complete the sheet.
You may choose to complete it together and discuss each item as you go.

Closure - Discussion for Insight
Review the idea of a closed system - if you know one element you know them all. Contrast this to the personal closed system of front, back, left and right where front changed according to the object's orientation. In this system, north is fixed and does not move with the orientation of the object.

Page 2

Things to Consider
The relationship of one direction to another must be well internalized.

Work on the Sheet
Students complete the sheet.

Closure - Discussion for Insight
Just as errors between front and back were rare while errors involving left and right were more common, errors between north and south are rare while errors involving east and west are more common.

Page 3

Things to Consider
Pages 3 – 5 place a human in the system much like the exercises in *Orientation in Space I*.
This task is similar to the task found on page two in *Orientation in Space I*.

Work on the Sheet
Students complete the sheet.

Closure - Discussion for Insight
It is helpful to compare a new (unfamiliar) system to an old (familiar) system to enhance understanding.

Page 4

Things to Consider
Pages 3 – 5 place a human in the system much like the exercises in *Orientation in Space I*.
This task is similar to the tasks found on pages 3 and 4 in *Orientation in Space I* (visual transport, using a table to organize information).

Work on the Sheet
Students complete the sheet.

Closure - Discussion for Insight
Discuss and evaluate strategies for work.

Page 5

Things to Consider
Pages 3 – 5 place a human in the system much like the exercises in *Orientation in Space I*.
This task is similar to the task found on page five in *Orientation in Space I* (flexibility in switching from one task to another).

Work on the Sheet
Students complete the sheet.

Closure - Discussion for Insight
Discuss and evaluate strategies for work. Note the difference in the tasks from page four to the tasks on this page. Tasks one and two are tasks of identification. Task three is more difficult because one of the givens is a relationship and the referent must be identified. Task four requires flexibility to switch tasks from line to line.

Page 6

Things to Consider
This page introduces turns as a way of getting oriented to a given position. Each turn is 90 degrees or a quarter turn.

Work on the Sheet
Students complete the sheet.

Closure - Discussion for Insight
Discuss: use of the term "turn." We understand turn as meaning 90 degrees or a quarter of a turn. So we're using the same word, turn, to mean 360 degrees and 90 degrees. It works because we have all agreed to the meaning.

Give examples of alternative methods that have the same result.

Page 7

Things to Consider
Doing and undoing.

Decode the same information verbally, numerically, and symbolically.

Work on the Sheet
Students complete the sheet.

Make sure students visualize themselves in the middle of the model at the intersection of the horizontal and vertical lines. Model some of the turns physically and make sure students are <u>pivoting</u>, not walking a curved path around the circle from point to point.

Closure - Discussion for Insight
What cancels each other out? Does it matter in what order it happens? Where can we do and undo things? For example, subtraction undoes addition, division undoes multiplication.

Page 8

Things to Consider
More practice with concepts from pages 6 and 7.
Make sure students visualize themselves in the middle of the model at the intersection of the horizontal and vertical lines and visualize a <u>pivot</u>, rather than a curved path around the circle from point to point.

Work on the Sheet
Students complete the sheet.

Closure - Discussion for Insight
We may use different sequences to arrive at the same goal. Generate examples such as learning/saving money for something special, learning a football play, or mastering a math algorithm.

Page 9

Things to Consider
Consider and use a two-coordinate grid. Most students are already proficient with the concept. Compare it to playing the game *Battleship*.

Work on the Sheet
Students work in pairs to complete the sheet.

Closure - Discussion for Insight
Discuss two ways of using the grid:
- name a spot using ordered pairs,(2,2)
- describe a spot in relation to another spot, (two spaces north and one space west)
-

Where are these ways used in life? GPS locations for the first, naming a spot. Giving directions can use either way (the house is at the intersection of Pine and Elm Streets or two blocks north of the library).

Pages 10 and 11

Things to Consider
These pages provide practice using a grid.

Work on the Sheet
Students complete page 11 using the grid on page 10.

Closure - Discussion for Insight
Possible discussion points:
- To solve a complex problem you must first become familiar with similar but simpler tasks or perform many simple tasks in the prescribed order (one step at time).
- You cannot predict the end of a journey by looking at the beginning (all five destinations on page 10 started at the same point).
- Checking off each step in a long, complex operation can be helpful so that nothing is forgotten, duplicated, or your place in the process is not lost. Generate examples such as packing for a vacation, Christmas shopping, or a pilot's checklist.
- A small error in the beginning may become greater over time and/or distance. Generate examples such as following a knitting pattern, building a house, being off one degree for a one mile trip compared to a thousand mile trip.

Page 12

Things to Consider
More practice with the grid. The tasks are the same as those on pages 10 and 11. Depending on the needs of your students you may choose to skip this page.

Work on the Sheet
Students complete the page.

Closure - Discussion for Insight
Continue with ideas from the discussion of pages 10 and 11.

Page 13

Things to Consider
Introduce the intermediate directions on a compass rose for more specificity.

Use a graphic organizer (table) to organize and record a large amount information.

Work on the Sheet
Students complete the sheet.

Closure - Discussion for Insight
Give examples of other situations that may or may not require more or less precision such as hours, minutes, and seconds. Name situations when each one is required. The degree of precision depends on one's needs.

Page 14

Things to Consider
Introduce 1/8 of a circle turn. (45 degrees)
Compare this page to page 7.
Explore combining steps using math.

Work on the Sheet
Students complete the sheet.

Closure - Discussion for Insight
Using math allows us to eliminate duplicate steps.
A simple problem prepares us for a similar, more complex problem.

Pages 15 and 16

Things to Consider
Page 15 is an AV page which sets the stage for page 16. You may choose to use both pages individually, use the pages together, or skip page 15 based on the needs of your students.

Use diagonals as well as vertical and horizontal paths on a grid system.

Translate from a verbal to a graphic modality and from a graphic to a verbal modality.

Work on the Sheet
On page 16, students work with a partner. Each student should have the opportunity to have the role of A and B. After completing the task, the students work together to analyze the results and check for error. If errors are found, the source of the error needs to be identified.

Closure - Discussion for Insight
Evaluate and give examples of the following ideas: (encourage divergent thinking – this isn't just about physical paths):

- Shortcuts can be beneficial. They can save time, energy, space or money. However, we must be sure a shortcut is the best option (give examples of when it is and when it isn't).
- How one arrives at a goal is as important as reaching the goal.
- When we know the path another has taken we can duplicate it.

There are two sources of error:
3. The written directions were not precise and complete.
4. The written directions were not followed accurately.

Page 17

Things to Consider
Explore a relative system of spatial reference with an absolute system (relative, westness or eastness).

Work on the Sheet
Students complete the sheet.

Closure - Discussion for Insight
One's relationship to a person, object, or event is determined by one's perspective. It changes with one's relative perspective. For example, the parent-child relationship changes when parents get older and depend on the child for help or the boss-employee relationship changes when both are on the committee outside of work and the employee is the chairperson of the committee.

Pages 18 - 20

Things to Consider
These pages are used together to sum up the instrument. Integrate an 8 point compass system, a grid system, and the relativity of an absolute system.

Work on the Sheet
Students complete the sheet.

Closure - Discussion for Insight
After students complete the pages discuss items they found interesting or challenging.
Summarize the instrument with a student-created graphic organizer.

IE Survival Guide
Transitive Relations

Goal
Transitive Relations is about equalities and inequalities.

Big Ideas:
- This instrument deals with symbolic representations of relationships requiring the use of abstractions and a higher level of thinking.
- The relationships exist in ordered pairs in which the differences between the sets are described as greater than, less than, or equal to.
- Strengthens the ability to infer new relationships from existing ones through hypothetical, inductive, and deductive thinking.
- Strengthens the learner's ability to respond to new learning. Rather than having the mindset "I can't do this. I've never seen this before." The mindset might be, "I will be able to come to a conclusion if I analyze the information and make some inferences."

There is so much potential for mediation on each page of this instrument. What follows are only suggestions. It is important to allow the students' to do their work and to let your observations drive the mediation. For example, if you plan to talk about precision but the students change strategies, notice the change in strategy and make the students aware of that change in strategy. There will be plenty of opportunity to talk about precision on another page.

Cover Page

In my experience, I have realized that I don't need to endlessly repeat the individual pieces of the cover page. In other words, don't spend so much time on each part that you lose students' interest. The following are constructs and ideas for potential discussions. Don't do them all at once since you will have two more opportunities (one for each instrument) to cover the salient points.

Logo (a thinker) - simple, memorable, visual (you may have the student put their picture here).
Discuss, "What does it mean to think?"
- Brainstorm: recalling, remembering, reflecting, making decisions, having ideas, solving problems, planning to do something, imagining, anticipating, and drawing conclusions.

Talk about problem solving. What is involved?
- Make a chart. Do this collectively with your students. Identify the problem, gather information (through our senses – give examples), consider possible courses of action/solutions, make a plan, carry out the plan, and check for accuracy.

Example: I use a hypothetical problem – I need to ride my bike but I can't. What's the problem? Is it the tire? The chain?

Title – *Transitive Relations*

Symbol - Ask the students what they notice. Invite them to hypothesize the meaning of the symbol (looks like elaboration in the brain and also notice the mathematical symbols). Between the input and output there must be an elaboration of the information. The conclusion is the result of a thought process.

Slogan - "Just a Moment . . . LET ME THINK!" This remains the same throughout all the Standard Instruments. It conveys an idea of calmness of the mind. We have time to think and thinking takes time. Some answers take more time to think through than others. It is normal/necessary to think before completing a task.

In *Mind Set* Carol Dweck says that people with fixed mind sets believe smart people already know and therefore don't need time to think. However, a person who has a growth mind set believes learning is a process which takes time and effort. This also helps with restraining impulsivity. Encourage students to think before they act/answer.

Page 1

Things to Consider
Review the signs for greater than and less than. Students use these symbols in math but on this page they are used for different kinds of ideas.

Work on the Sheet
You may want to do this page together as a class and discuss the examples as you work.

Closure - Discussion for Insight
We can compare and rank according to many different parameters. *(Comparisons)*

In the verbal modality, the word that expresses the relationship (greater than, less than, equal to) changes with the change in the referent. The signs, however, only change their direction and can be read from either direction.

The signs for size or magnitude do not describe the individual item but only the relationship between it and another item. For example, saying the red pencil is longer than the blue pencil does not mean the red pencil is long.

Page 2

Things to Consider
This is an AV page that reviews the concepts of greater than, less than, and equal to. Depending on the needs of your students, you may or may not choose to use it.

Work on the Sheet
Students complete the page.

Closure - Discussion for Insight
To order items according to size, power, or magnitude, locate them relative to one another so that the relationship between them is conserved regardless of the direction they are ranked.

Page 3

Things to Consider
Introduce the signs for equal and not equal.

Work on the Sheet
The sign for equal is familiar from math and the concept is familiar to that found in *Comparisons*.

Closure - Discussion for Insight
Equivalency means having the same value. Items can be equivalent in one or more characteristics yet not equivalent in others. Give examples such as a pound of feathers and a pound of iron.
Also discuss examples from the bottom of the page such as king and president (can be equal in some characteristics). Both may have an equal highest rank in their respective governments yet their roles are very different.

In an ordered set, inequality does not express a rank – it is impossible to know the value of the items. For example, the statement "X does not equal 5," does not tell us which is greater or less than.

Page 4

Things to Consider
Introduce a symbol to symbolize not having enough information to reach a conclusion. Please point out to the students that this is not a universal symbol but is agreed upon for this instrument. By contrast, greater than, less than, and equal signs are universal symbols.

Work on the Sheet
Students complete the page.

Closure - Discussion for Insight
Discuss the difference between "I don't know" and "It is impossible to know." Sometimes we don't have enough information to draw a solid conclusion.

Page 5

Things to Consider
Practice using signs, words, and abbreviations.

Work on the Sheet
Students complete the page.

Closure - Discussion for Insight
Which is easier for you to use - the sign, words, or abbreviation? Why?

Page 6

Things to Consider
Using symbols, words, and abbreviations in a table to define implications of given relationships between two members of an ordered set.

Work on the Sheet
This page is incredibly complex. You may want to work through it together while discussing strategies and implications.

Closure - Discussion for Insight
Discuss strategies such as systematic work, paying attention to detail, or holding more than one piece of information at a time.

Make sure students start with the first column. If the conditions in the first column are true, can the conditions of the subsequent columns be correct, possible, or incorrect? Define the terms: correct means *always* correct, possible means it may or may not be correct under different conditions (for example, if A is not equal to B is A greater than B – it might be but it doesn't have to be – it's possible), incorrect means it can't be.

It is possible to express the same things in words, abbreviations, or symbols (signs). Although signs are the most abstract, they are sometimes the easiest and most efficient way to show complex problems.

Page 7

Things to Consider
This page is similar to page six but involves using <u>two</u> statements regarding the relationship between two members of an ordered set.

Work on the Sheet
This is an extremely complex page and depends on mastery of page 6. You may want to work through this task as a class or let confident students work independently while you work with less confident students.

Closure - Discussion for Insight
Discuss difficulties encountered. Were they caused at the input, elaboration, or output phase?

Discuss ways of thinking to infer and draw conclusions from the given statements.

Page 8

Things to Consider
Introduce the idea of transitivity: transferable that which is from one pair of terms to another. This page transfers equality (these ideas are worked on in pages 8 – 12).

Work on the Sheet
Assign letters to the terms in the problems. #3 weight of salt (A), weight of sugar (B), weight of a sack and a half of flour (C)

Students are seeking valid conclusions based on the given information. The information in the statements is not open to argument. For example, #4 a student thinks coffee not as sweet as cocoa. That is not open for discussion. We use the given information as fact to draw conclusions.

Closure - Discussion for Insight
The structure of transitivity includes two statements being given and a third statement with a conclusion inferred from the implications of the first two statements and the transfer of the relationships.
In order for the transfer of relationships to happen three conditions must exist:
1. The items must all be part of the same ordered set and ranked according to the same attribute (in these examples items are ranked according to weight, speed, age, taste, or number).
2. The relationships must be expressed in terms of greater than, less than or equal to (in these examples they are all equal).
3. There must be a common item in the two statements through which the relationship can be transferred.

Page 9

Things to Consider
Repeated work with the idea of transitivity. This page transfers greater than relationships.

Work on the Sheet
Have the student work on the sheet.

Closure - Discussion for Insight
The structure of transitivity includes:
- two statements being given
- a third statement with a conclusion inferred from the implications of the first two statements and the transfer of the relationships

In order for the transfer of relationships to happen three conditions must exist:
1. The items must all be part of the same ordered set and ranked according to the same attribute (in these examples items are ranked according to weight, speed, age, taste, or number).
2. The relationships must be expressed in terms of greater than, less than or equal to (in these examples they are all equal).
3. There must be a common item in the two statements through which the relationship can be transferred.

Page 10

Things to Consider
Repeated work with the idea of transitivity. This page transfers the relationships between members of an ordered set when there is a common member but the given relationships between the members are different.

Work on the Sheet
Students complete the page.

Closure - Discussion for Insight
The structure of transitivity includes:
- two statements being given
- a third statement with a conclusion inferred from the implications of the first two statements and the transfer of the relationships

In order for the transfer of relationships to happen three conditions must exist:
1. The items must all be part of the same ordered set and ranked according to the same attribute (in these examples items are ranked according to weight, speed, age, taste, or number).
2. The relationships must be expressed in terms of greater than, less than or equal to (in these examples they are all equal).
3. There must be a common item in the two statements through which the relationship can be transferred.

When two items are equal one may be substituted for the other.

Page 11

Things to Consider
This page is much like page 10 with different relationships in the statements.

Work on the Sheet
Students complete the page.

Closure - Discussion for Insight
The structure of transitivity includes:
- two statements being given
- a third statement with a conclusion inferred from the implications of the first two statements and the transfer of the relationships

In order for the transfer of relationships to happen three conditions must exist:
1. The items must all be part of the same ordered set and ranked according to the same attribute (in these examples items are ranked according to weight, speed, age, taste, or number).
2. The relationships must be expressed in terms of greater than, less than or equal to (in these examples they are all equal).
3. There must be a common item in the two statements through which the relationship can be transferred.

The order of the <u>statements</u> expressing relationships in an ordered set is irrelevant.

Page 12

Things to Consider
This is a review of the previous pages (8 – 11). Although this is an AV page I would not recommend skipping it.

Work on the Sheet
Flexibility is shown by switching tasks from example to example.

Closure - Discussion for Insight
Example 10 creates a paradox. No formal logical conclusion can be drawn using the formulas we have learned. We know that 7 is less than 12 and 12 is less than 24, yet we have no logical conclusion that can be reached using transitive rules. Note: the paradox can be solved by writing the relationship like this:
C is less than A
A is less than B
Therefore: C is less than B

By ordering the items like this we have A as the middle term through which the relationships can be transferred.

Page 13

Things to Consider
Understand the conditions under which relationships in ordered sets cannot be determined.

Work on the Sheet
Students complete the page.

Closure - Discussion for Insight
The inability to draw conclusions is not due to the students' inability or failure but rather due to certain conditions not being met in the problem.

Page 14

Things to Consider
Compare the formula on the top of this page to the formula at the top of page 9.

Work on the Sheet
Students complete the page.

Closure - Discussion for Insight
When no information is given or known about the dimension for ordering, a conclusion can still be reached by using the rules of transitivity. For example, on task 4 we don't know in what way Mike (A) is less than Jon (B) (it might be that he weighs less, is younger, makes a lower salary). But we can still draw the conclusion that David is greater than Mike.

Page 15

Things to Consider
Draw conclusions regarding the order of individual terms in an equation.

Work on the Sheet
Students complete the page.

Closure - Discussion for Insight
In the box it appears only two statements are given:
1. $A + B > A + C$
2. $B\ ?\ C$

The third statement is implied: $A = A$

When the same term appears in both statements of an equation it has no effect on the given relationship. Its effect in the one expression is cancelled by the effect in the other expression. Therefore, any difference between the two expressions of the equation is the result of the remaining terms of the expression.

Page 16

Things to Consider
Analyze an equation to determine if transitivity is possible from the given relationship between the two expressions.
1. The equation looks similar to the one on page 15 (A + B › A + C) but this time we want to know the relationship between A and C

Work on the Sheet
Students complete the page.

Closure - Discussion for Insight
It is impossible to draw conclusions when the question involves two terms from the same expression in the equation.

Page 17

Things to Consider
Draw conclusions in an equation based on equality.

Work on the Sheet
Students complete the page.

Closure - Discussion for Insight
Discuss the conditions necessary for drawing a conclusion. Are these conditions met in the examples on this page?

Page 18

Things to Consider
Expand and consolidate the concepts necessary to draw conclusions regarding relationships between terms in equivalent expressions.

Work on the Sheet
Students complete the page.

Closure - Discussion for Insight
It is possible to conserve the <u>equality</u> between <u>two expressions</u> under the following conditions:
- When a term in one expression equals a term in the other expression, the two remaining terms are also equal.
- When a term in one expression is larger than a term in the other expression (A › C), its companion must be smaller than the remaining term in the other expression (B ‹ D)
- When a term in one expression is larger than a term in the other expression (A › C), its companion must be smaller than the remaining term in the other expression (B ‹ D)

Page 19

Things to Consider
Analyze the given equation to understand why it is impossible to know the relationship between its terms.

Work on the Sheet
Students complete the page.

Closure - Discussion for Insight
There are many possibilities that can/will fit the given equation.

Page 20

Things to Consider
Consolidate and practice drawing valid conclusions.

Work on the Sheet
Students work on the sheet.

Closure - Discussion for Insight
In order to draw valid conclusions, all the information must be considered in order to determine whether or not it permits the transfer of relationships.

Pages 21 and 22

Things to Consider
Learn to seek information necessary for the transfer of relationships.

Work on the Sheet
The equation at the top of the page differs from previous equations in that the value of the two C's in the one expression are known to be equal. That permits the transfer of relationships in certain instances.

Closure - Discussion for Insight
In verbal problems, one must read carefully to determine what is being asked, what information is relevant, and what relationships are given. Using symbols and signs raises the level of abstraction but also eliminates confusion caused by order of presentation or irrelevant details. The statement written in symbols and signs makes it easy to see whether or not the relationships are transitive.

Pages 23 and 24

Things to Consider
These two pages are summary pages. Students must encode information given verbally and decode information given in signs and symbols to draw conclusions based on the transfer of relationships.

Work on the Sheet
Students complete the pages.
No formulas or equations are given on these pages. The students are asked to make inferences based on the rules, relationships, and implications learned in the instrument.

Closure - Discussion for Insight
Students should summarize the instrument by constructing a graphic organizer showing all the ideas, rules, strategies and principles learned in the instrument.

IE Survival Guide
Syllogisms

<u>Goal</u>
Syllogisms is similar to *Transitive Relations* in that students will learn to infer new relationships from existing ones in order to draw logical conclusions. While *Transitive Relations* dealt with pairs of things and their relationships with regards to greater than, less than, or equal to, *Syllogisms* involves sets and set theory – how members of sets are related to each other.

<u>Big Ideas:</u>
- The tasks in *Syllogisms* require comparing, categorization, encoding, decoding, inferential thinking, and hypothetical and deductive reasoning.
- Some of the set theory ideas include
    o Some sets are exclusive: no member of Set A is a member of Set B
    o Subsets exist in which all members of Set B are members of Set A but not all members of Set A are members of Set B
    o There are intersecting sets in which some members of Set A are members of Set B
- In *Syllogisms* one must consider the truth of the propositions used to draw conclusions. There is a difference between "true" and "valid." Truth depends on whether the propositions are true where validity depends on the argument. In *Syllogisms* we are concerned with validity.

There is so much potential for mediation on each page of this instrument. These are only suggestions. It is important to let what the students are doing and let your noticing drive the mediation. For example, if you plan to talk about precision but the students change strategies, notice the change in strategy and make the students aware of that. There will be plenty of opportunity to talk about precision on another page.

Cover Page

In my experience, I have found that you don't need to beat the individual pieces of the cover page to death. In other words don't spend so much time on each part that you lose students' interest. The following are potential discussions. Don't do them all at once. You've already had 12 opportunities and you still have one more chance (one for each instrument) after this one to cover salient points.

Logo (a thinker) - simple, memorable, visual (you may have the student put their picture here)
Discuss "What does it mean to think?"
- Brainstorm: recalling, remembering, reflecting, making decisions, having ideas, solving problems, planning to do something, imagining, anticipating, and drawing conclusions.

Talk about problem solving. What is involved?
- Make a chart: get students to list: identify the problem, gather information – (through our senses – give examples) consider possible courses of action/solutions, make a plan, carry out the plan, check for accuracy

Example: I use a hypothetical problem – I need to ride my bike but I can't: What's the problem? Is it the tire? The chain?

Title – *Syllogisms*

Symbol - Ask the students what they notice. Invite them to hypothesize the meaning of the symbol (Venn diagram with extra part, we can use models to help us understand complex information).

Slogan - "Just a Moment . . . LET ME THINK!" This stays the same throughout all the Standard Instruments. It conveys an idea of calmness of the mind. We have time to think and thinking takes time. Some answers take more time to think about than others. It is normal/necessary to think before completing a task.

In *Mind Set* Carol Dweck says that people with fixed mind sets believe smart people already know and therefore don't need time to think. However, a person who has a growth mind set believes learning is a process which takes time and effort. This also helps with restraining impulsivity. Encourage students to think before they act/ answer.

Page 1

Things to Consider
Develop a concept of set

Work on the Sheet
Students complete the page.

Closure - Discussion for Insight
Discuss the idea of finding "just right sized words."
Discuss similarities with *Categorizations*. An item can't be both part of a set and not part of the set (just as items couldn't be part of a category and not part of a category). Just as it is possible to categorize and re-categorize things, set membership can change depending on the definition of the set.

Page 2

Things to Consider
Categorize things into sets. Use the term "member" to label one item in a set.

Work on the Sheet
Students complete the page.

Closure - Discussion for Insight
A circle is used to show the boundaries of a set. Members that belong are inside the circle, members that do not belong are outside the circle. An item must be either in or out of the circle. There are no members "on the line."

Membership in a set depends on the definition of the set and meeting the criteria.

The more criteria defining a set, the less members in the set. For example, if the criteria were: must be a counting number, must be even, must be divisible by 8 – for each additional condition or criteria, members were eliminated.

The same items can be members of different sets. For example, the number two is part of the set of even numbers and the set of counting numbers.

Page 3

Things to Consider
More practice determining set membership.
Recognize the difference between inductive and deductive thinking.

Work on the Sheet
Students complete the page.

Closure - Discussion for Insight
Deductive thinking - given a generalization think of examples
Inductive thinking - given specific examples, think of the generalization

Page 4

Things to Consider
Introduce syllogisms: draw a conclusion based on a simple deductive statement.

Work on the Sheet
Students complete the page.

Closure - Discussion for Insight
You may need to discuss and reinforce the vocabulary: set, member, and trait.

A syllogism contains two propositions and one conclusion. It is important to use the vocabulary of syllogisms for clear and precise communication.

Conclusions are drawn based on the implications of the given statements: if... then.

Be sure to discuss the summary at the bottom of the page – it explains the structure of a basic syllogism.

Page 5

Things to Consider
A syllogism is not about truth, it is about logic (validity).

Work on the Sheet
Students complete the page.

Closure - Discussion for Insight
The conclusion in a syllogism is reached by inference from the implications of the two given statements. A statement may be logically true, but still be false. For example, if a proposition is false, a false statement can be logically true. Given the two propositions: All snakes are poisonous. and A garter snake is a snake. The logical conclusion is A garter snake is poisonous.

Start talking about the affect this has on arguments in the world. People argue based on propositions which may or may not be true. The logical conclusions may be solid but different people arrive at different logical conclusions based on their propositions. Propositions based on stereotypes can be especially problematic. You will continue this conversation throughout the rest of this instrument. Examples may include environmental issues – do cloth diapers really save the environment? There will be fewer disposable diapers in the landfills but how much more water, detergent, and energy was used for laundering the cloth diapers?
Ethanol – fossil fuels used in growing the crops compared to fossil fuel not consumed in vehicles
Wind turbines
Social issues – immigration policies, health care

Link the discussion to conflicts that come up in other content area, especially social studies and science.

Page 6

Things to Consider
Define exclusive sets (they do not have a single member in common).

Work on the Sheet
Students complete the page.

Closure - Discussion for Insight
Sets must be well defined.

Page 7

Things to Consider
More practice with exclusive sets.

Work on the Sheet
Students complete the page.

Closure - Discussion for Insight

Page 8

Things to Consider
Syllogism for exclusive sets.

Work on the Sheet
Students complete the page.

Closure - Discussion for Insight
Syllogisms based on exclusive sets are easily recognized by the word "no." (No A is B)

Page 9

Things to Consider
Define identical sets (when all members of set A also belong to set B).

Work on the Sheet
Students complete the page.

Closure - Discussion for Insight
Some sets appear to be identical but are not. One must be careful to ensure that the sets are actually identical. The relationship must be symmetrical in order to be identical. For example, all A is B means that all B must be A.

Page 10

Things to Consider
More work with identical sets.

Work on the Sheet
Students complete the page.

Closure - Discussion for Insight
Even if there is only one exception, the sets are not identical. Knowing that two sets are identical allows us to transfer any conclusions about one set to the other.

Page 11

Things to Consider
Define subsets as well-defined parts of larger universal sets. This concept has already been introduced in *Categorizations*.

Work on the Sheet
Students complete the page.

Closure - Discussion for Insight
A Venn diagram is a useful tool to show sets and subsets.
Traits of the universal set are shared by members of the subset. Some members of the universal set are members of the subset. All members of the subset are members of the universal set.

Page 12

Things to Consider
Learn the symbol for showing subsets.

Work on the Sheet
Students complete the page.

Closure - Discussion for Insight
The opening in the symbol always faces the larger inclusive set.

Page 13

Things to Consider
Present information regarding sets and subsets using different modalities.

Work on the Sheet
Students complete the page.

Closure - Discussion for Insight
You may want to have your students show the information at the bottom of the page with Venn diagrams as well.

Page 14

Things to Consider
Use syllogistic reasoning and inferential thinking.

Work on the Sheet
Students complete the page.

Closure - Discussion for Insight
Think about sets and subsets – which is which.
Talk about the non-verbal modality of examples 4 and 5. Does that make the task easier or more difficult?
Talk about how drawing the diagram can be helpful.

Page 15

Things to Consider
Pages 15 and 16 review principles of classification that were introduced in *Categorizations*. They provide practice in assigning items to universal sets, subsets, and exclusive sets.

Work on the Sheet
Students complete the page.

Closure - Discussion for Insight
Using Venn diagrams helps us see relationships between subsets and universal sets quickly and precisely.

It is essential to use the same principles of classification and the same attribute in each phase of categorization. Review from *Categorizations* but shown in a different context.

Page 16

Things to Consider
Pages 15 and 16 review principles of classification that were introduced in *Categorizations*. They provide practice in assigning items to universal sets, subsets, and exclusive sets.

Work on the Sheet
Students complete the page.

Closure - Discussion for Insight
Continue discussion from work on page 15 and any other issues that arose during work on this page.

Page 17

Things to Consider
Page 17 is and AV page reviewing sets, subsets, nested sets, and exclusive sets. I would not skip this page.

Work on the Sheet
Students complete the page.

Closure - Discussion for Insight
Discuss the variety of relationships that exist between the sets and subsets.

Page 18

Things to Consider
Represent the same information in two different graphic organizers which help us recognize sets and subsets.

Work on the Sheet
Students complete the page.

Closure - Discussion for Insight
Continue discussing the variety of relationships that exist between the sets and subsets. You might want to ask students: "What did you find interesting?"

Page 19

Things to Consider
Draw conclusions based on the relationships between sets.

Work on the Sheet
Students complete the page.
This page is difficult to talk about since it is made up of symbols. In order to talk about it you need to label the symbols.

Closure - Discussion for Insight
Talk about our inability to discuss until we have labeled. For symbols without a universal label, it doesn't matter what we call them as long as we all agree. This concept was first introduced in *Organization of Dots*.

Page 20

Things to Consider
Review the principles of classification – classify the same sets according to different criteria.

Work on the Sheet
Students complete the page.

Closure - Discussion for Insight
Ask students to discuss what they found interesting on this page.

Page 21

Things to Consider
More work with universal sets, subsets, and the relationship between them.

Work on the Sheet
Students complete the page.

Closure - Discussion for Insight
Using symbols (as in example 5) allows us to look at the relationship only and not let other knowledge about objects get in the way of making a logical conclusion.

Page 22

Things to Consider
Introduce intersecting sets.

Work on the Sheet
Students complete the page.

Closure - Discussion for Insight
Discuss naming the intersecting set.

Page 23

Things to Consider
Name universal sets and subsets formed at the intersection of two universal sets.

Work on the Sheet
Students complete the page.

Closure - Discussion for Insight
The members of the intersecting set have characteristics from both the universal sets. The name for the intersecting set should indicate the universal set it came from. The order of the label is not important except perhaps for efficiency ("even numbers divisible by 3" or "numbers divisible by 3 that are even").

Page 24

Things to Consider

Name universal sets and subsets formed at the intersection of two universal sets.

Work on the Sheet

Students complete the page.

Closure - Discussion for Insight

Continue the discussion from page 23. The members of the intersecting set have characteristics from both the universal sets. The name for the intersecting set should indicate the universal set it came from. The order of the label is not important except perhaps for efficiency ("even numbers divisible by 3" or "numbers divisible by 3 that are even"). Generate more examples.

Page 25

Things to Consider
Use Venn diagrams to encode verbal information.

Work on the Sheet
Students complete the page.

Closure - Discussion for Insight
Discuss the pros and cons of the Venn diagram compared to the verbal modality.

Page 26

Things to Consider
This is an AV page.
Use Venn diagrams to encode graphic information.

Work on the Sheet
Students complete the page.

Closure - Discussion for Insight
This might remind students of page 1 in *Analytic Perceptions*.

Page 27

Things to Consider
This is an AV page. It gives opportunity to draw conclusions from relationships of intersecting sets starting with verbal examples and going to abstract symbols.

Work on the Sheet
Students complete the page.

Closure - Discussion for Insight
Ask students to generate their own examples. For example: "I am a fifth grader at City Elementary School. I attend at City Elementary School. Am I a fifth grader?

Pages 28 and 29

Things to Consider
On these pages we expand the ideas of intersecting sets by using three universal sets and Venn diagrams to encode the information.

Work on the Sheet
Students complete the pages.

Closure - Discussion for Insight
Discuss strategies: With complex work we need to work systematically.
Discuss any misconceptions about set theory that may arise.

Pages 30 and 31

Things to Consider
More work with three intersecting sets.

Work on the Sheet
Students complete the page.

Closure - Discussion for Insight
Discuss the need to be careful not to overgeneralize.

Page 32

Things to Consider
This page explores a different way for three sets to intersect. A Venn diagram is used to encode the information.

Work on the Sheet
Students complete the page.

Closure - Discussion for Insight
Discuss when using a model like this is appropriate and when logically two sets will not intersect. For example, birds, fish, and creatures I have seen in person – birds and fish are exclusive sets.

Pages 33 and 34

Things to Consider
The work up to this point has been about developing concepts surrounding set theory. Starting on page 33 the focus is on syllogisms. Two propositions are given and the third is a conclusion which can be logically drawn from the relationship given between the two elements but not directly linked in the two propositions.

Work on the Sheet
Students complete the pages.

Closure - Discussion for Insight
The conclusions in syllogisms must be logically derived. Some propositions do not lead to a logical conclusion.

Page 35

Things to Consider
Draw conclusions about set membership using given statements.

Work on the Sheet
Students complete the page.

Closure - Discussion for Insight
Ask students what they found interesting about his page.

Pages 36 and 37

Things to Consider
Practice drawing conclusions from syllogisms that contain intersections of two universal sets where one is a subset that is also intersected.

Work on the Sheet
Students complete the page.

Closure - Discussion for Insight
When a set intersects with the subset of another set, it also intersects with the universal set of that subset.

Page 38

Things to Consider
This is an AV page. Use it to summarize the instrument.

Work on the Sheet
Students complete the page.

Closure - Discussion for Insight
Discuss all the important ideas from the instrument.

IE Survival Guide
Representational Stencil Design

Goal
Representational Stencil Design contains the most complex tasks of any of the instruments because the whole task is mental. There is no motor manipulation – all tasks are done in the mind and visualized with no possibility of trial and error to observe and evaluate results.

This instrument is an excellent tool to summarize the Instrumental Enrichment program. Be sure to bridge back to other instruments as you go through it.

Big Ideas:
Representational Stencil Design requires the use of all strategies and thinking skills developed though the previous instruments.
- Precision, restraint of impulsivity, using more than one source of information at a time, determining what is relevant and irrelevant (used in all the instruments)
- Recognizing and duplicating a model (*Organization of Dots*)
- Noticing similarities and differences (*Comparisons*)
- Analyze and synthesize parts of the model to break a complex task into parts (*Analytic Perception*)
- Ability to see things from different perspectives *Orientation in Space I and II*)
- Sequencing (both temporal and spatial) (*Temporal Relations*)

There is so much potential for mediation on each page of this instrument. What follows are only suggestions. It is important to allow the students' to do work and to let your observations drive the mediation. For example, if you plan to talk about precision but the students change strategies, note the change in strategy and make the students aware of that change in strategy. There will be plenty of opportunities to talk about precision on another page.

Cover Page

In my experience, I have found that you don't need to beat the individual pieces of the cover page to death. In other words don't spend so much time on each part that you lose students' interest. The following are potential discussions.

Logo (a thinker) - simple, memorable, visual (you may have the student put their picture here)
Discuss "What does it mean to think?"
- Brainstorm: recalling, remembering, reflecting, making decisions, having ideas, solving problems, planning to do something, imagining, anticipating, and drawing conclusions.

Talk about problem solving. What is involved?
- Make a chart: get students to list: identify the problem, gather information (through our senses – give examples) consider possible courses of action/solutions, make a plan, carry out the plan, and check for accuracy.

Example: I use a hypothetical problem – I need to ride my bike but I can't: What's the problem? Is it the tire? The chain?

Title – *Representational Stencil Design*

Symbol - Ask the students what they notice. Invite them to hypothesize the meaning of the symbol.

Slogan - "Just a Moment . . . LET ME THINK!" This stays the same throughout all the Standard Instruments. It conveys an idea of calmness of the mind. We have time to think and thinking takes time. Some answers take more time to think about than others. It is normal/necessary to think before completing a task.

In *Mind Set* Carol Dweck says that people with fixed mind sets believe smart people already know and therefore don't need time to think. However, a person who has a growth mind set believes learning is a process which takes time and effort. This also helps with restraining impulsivity. Encourage students to think before they act/ answer.

Page 1

Things to Consider
This page is used to familiarize the students with the stencils which will be used throughout the instrument (categorize the stencils according to different attributes).

Work on the Sheet
Students complete the page.

Closure - Discussion for Insight
Discuss, "How does categorization help organize something which seems complex." There are a lot of stencils, but when you start grouping them, they are easier to remember.

Page 2

Things to Consider
Categorize and re-categorize the stencils using different principles of classification.

Work on the Sheet
Students complete the page.

Closure - Discussion for Insight
Perception of order is impossible when items are isolated or in disarray.

Bridge to real life – it is impossible to know how many outfits you have if clothing is in a heap at the bottom of the closet.

Pages 3 and 4

Things to Consider
More practice categorizing and re-categorizing stencils using numbers as labels for each stencil.

Work on the Sheet
Students complete the page.

Closure - Discussion for Insight
These pages might seem a bit redundant but you must build familiarity with the stencils. Familiarity with the stencils will be helpful when doing the more difficult work.

Page 5

Things to Consider
Analyze designs made by combining stencils.

This page introduces the way we will encode the tasks (stencil number separated by a dash with the numbers written in the order they are applied from the bottom up).

Work on the Sheet
Students complete the page.

Closure - Discussion for Insight
What is the importance of our encoding system?

Bridge to *Analytic Perceptions* - the whole is formed of parts that are wholes. The new whole is the result of the combination (interaction – masking and unmasking) of the component wholes.

Page 6

Things to Consider
Page 6 is an AV page. It reviews the ideas developed so far and is an error correction page.

Work on the Sheet
Students complete the page.

Closure - Discussion for Insight
Review ideas about error correction (*Organization of Dots*)
- Errors of omission
- Errors of commission
- One must discover the source of an error in order to fix it or avoid it in the future

Page 7

Things to Consider
Pages 7 through 25 work through the solutions to stencil designs 1 – 55. The strategies and relevant ideas change from page to page but many of the ideas remain the same:
- Making a hypothesis and checking it
- Proving a solution through logic
- Using clear communication to explain and persuade

This page deals with stencil designs 1 – 4.
Notice – on the first stencil designs it may be possible to "see" the solution. Pay attention to the process. As the designs get more complex, the process will become essential when the solution can no longer be "seen."

Work on the Sheet
Students complete the page.

Closure - Discussion for Insight
The possible errors described in #4 are the same for the whole instrument.

Page 8

Things to Consider
Pages 7 through 25 work through the solutions to stencil designs 1 – 55. The strategies and relevant ideas change from page to page but many of the ideas remain the same:
- Making a hypothesis and checking it
- Proving a solution through logic
- Using clear communication to explain and persuade

This page deals with stencil designs 5 and 6.

Work on the Sheet
Students complete the page.

Closure - Discussion for Insight
The method of encoding is reviewed.

A forced choice limits the alternatives. For example, color limits possible stencils which can be chosen. When is this true in life? Multiple choice tests – you think you know the answer but that answer doesn't appear in the choices. You want to watch a show on TV but your choice is preempted by a speech by the president.

Page 9

Things to Consider
Pages 7 through 25 work through the solutions to stencil designs 1 – 55. The strategies and relevant ideas change from page to page but many of the ideas remain the same:
- Making a hypothesis and checking it
- Proving a solution through logic
- Using clear communication to explain and persuade

This page deals with stencil designs 7 - 10.
Notice – Whenever stencils 3, 4, or 8 are used the stencils beneath them appear twice making it appear that two stencils have been used.

Work on the Sheet
Students complete the page.

Closure - Discussion for Insight
There can be a difference between what one sees and what one knows.

Page 10

Things to Consider
Pages 7 through 25 work through the solutions to stencil designs 1 – 55. The strategies and relevant ideas change from page to page but many of the ideas remain the same:
- Making a hypothesis and checking it
- Proving a solution through logic
- Using clear communication to explain and persuade

This page deals with stencil designs 11 – 14.
Notice – # 11 can be done with logic without looking at the design at all (if there is one error in each – first must be missing stencil, last must be extra stencil, middle must be wrong sequence [based on sequence in 1st and 3rd example)

Work on the Sheet
Students complete the page.

Closure - Discussion for Insight
This is another error page. Remember the possible errors that are described on page 7, #4.

Page 11

Things to Consider
Pages 7 through 25 work through the solutions to stencil designs 1 – 55. The strategies and relevant ideas change from page to page but many of the ideas remain the same:
- Making a hypothesis and checking it
- Proving a solution through logic
- Using clear communication to explain and persuade

This page deals with stencil designs 15 –17.
Notice – fusion of color. Distinguish what we see and what we know.

Work on the Sheet
Students complete the page.

Closure - Discussion for Insight
There is a difference between seeing and understanding.
- We can see without understanding: watching television (I enjoy the picture but I don't understand how it is generated); patterns in nature – I see and enjoy them but I don't understand why the patterns occur
- I can understand without seeing: bacteria causes illness but I can't see bacteria

Page 12

Things to Consider
Pages 7 through 25 work through the solutions to stencil designs 1 – 55. The strategies and relevant ideas change from page to page but many of the ideas remain the same:
- Making a hypothesis and checking it
- Proving a solution through logic
- Using clear communication to explain and persuade

This page deals with stencil designs 18 and 19.

Notice – This is an AV page that is similar to content found on to page 11, but your students will probably want to do this page it so that at the end of the instrument they will have completed all the designs.

Work on the Sheet
Students complete the page.

Closure - Discussion for Insight
What we see and what we know.

Pages 13 and 14

Things to Consider
Pages 7 through 25 work through the solutions to stencil designs 1 – 55. The strategies and relevant ideas change from page to page but many of the ideas remain the same:
- Making a hypothesis and checking it
- Proving a solution through logic
- Using clear communication to explain and persuade

I would teach these pages together since page 14 only has one stencil design and they are dealing with the same idea – fusion of color.
These pages deal with stencil designs 20 - 24.
Notice affects the circle has on design (#20, 21, 23) and orientation of the squares (#23).

Work on the Sheet
Students complete the page.

Closure - Discussion for Insight
When there is a fusion of color such as in design 21 with stencils 3 and 4 it doesn't matter which stencil is applied first. We may agree to list them in number order.

Page 15

Things to Consider
Pages 7 through 25 work through the solutions to stencil designs 1 – 55. The strategies and relevant ideas change from page to page but many of the ideas remain the same:
- Making a hypothesis and checking it
- Proving a solution through logic
- Using clear communication to explain and persuade

This page deals with stencil designs 25 - 27.
Notice – devise a strategy for testing hypotheses (#26 and 27).

Work on the Sheet
Students complete the page.

Closure - Discussion for Insight

Page 16

Things to Consider
Pages 7 through 25 work through the solutions to stencil designs 1 – 55. The strategies and relevant ideas change from page to page but many of the ideas remain the same:
- Making a hypothesis and checking it
- Proving a solution through logic
- Using clear communication to explain and persuade

This page deals with stencil designs 28 and 29.
Notice – use the orientation of the cut out square as the discriminator between stencils 16 and 17 and the orientation of the cut out crosses as the discriminator between stencils 3 and 4 (design 29).

Work on the Sheet
Students complete the page.

Closure - Discussion for Insight

Page 17

Things to Consider
Pages 7 through 25 work through the solutions to stencil designs 1 – 55. The strategies and relevant ideas change from page to page but many of the ideas remain the same:
- Making a hypothesis and checking it
- Proving a solution through logic
- Using clear communication to explain and persuade

This page deals with stencil designs 30 - 32.
Notice – gain efficiency by treating a part as if it were a whole (#30 – describe the pattern achieved by the two stencils in combination. This can also be seen on #29, page 16).

Work on the Sheet
Students complete the page.

Closure - Discussion for Insight
In convergence there is a total blending of two or more elements involved. Generate examples – blend voices or instruments in music, or blend paint in art.

Pages 18 - 20

Things to Consider
Pages 7 through 25 work through the solutions to stencil designs 1 – 55. The strategies and relevant ideas change from page to page but many of the ideas remain the same:
- Making a hypothesis and checking it
- Proving a solution through logic
- Using clear communication to explain and persuade

These pages deal with stencil designs 33 – 40.
Notice – more work with convergence

Work on the Sheet
Students complete the page.

Closure - Discussion for Insight
Discuss strategies, arguments, hypothetical thinking, etc. as it is applicable. Let the students generate the conversation.

Page 21

Things to Consider
Pages 21 – 25 deal with designs 41 – 55. The complexity increases in these designs. Some of the elements seem impossible to achieve with the limited stencils available.
Notice design 21 (the sequence of converging stencils does not matter).

Work on the Sheet
Students complete the page.

Closure - Discussion for Insight
Substitutes that are equivalent in function may or may not be similar in appearance to the items they replace. For example, you run out of green paint so you mix yellow and blue. Will the result be an exact match? You use white cake mix in a recipe instead of yellow cake mix, banana pudding instead of vanilla pudding. You can't find the scissors so you use a knife.

Page 22

Things to Consider
Pages 21 – 25 deal with designs 41 – 55. The complexity increases in these designs. Some of the elements seem impossible to achieve with the limited stencils available.
Notice: designs 43 – 45 contain converging stencils where order does not matter.

Work on the Sheet
Students complete the page.

Closure – Discussion for Insight
Experience and practice make a complex task easier.

Page 23

Things to Consider
Pages 21 – 25 deal with designs 41 – 55. The complexity increases in these designs. Some of the elements seem impossible to achieve with the limited stencils available.
Notice design 48 – compares designs which involve masking and convergence.

Work on the Sheet
Students complete the page.

Closure - Discussion for Insight
In most tasks, you can use a strategy where you accomplish the easy parts first and finish the rest. You may or may not need to devote more time to the second part. Sometimes getting the easy part out of the way makes the rest of the task easier. Generate examples such as taking a test (skip the hard problems, then coming back to them) doing home (use the same strategy).

Page 24

Things to Consider
Pages 21 – 25 deal with designs 41 – 55. The complexity is increases in these designs. Some of the elements seem impossible to achieve with the limited stencils available.
Notice designs 49 -52 compare designs which involve masking and convergence.

Work on the Sheet
Students complete the page.

Closure - Discussion for Insight
Phenomena which have no ready explanation can be explained by applying reasoning or rules. Generate examples such as jets (heavier than air but can still fly), ships (heavier than water but can still float)

Page 25

Things to Consider
Pages 21 – 25 deal with designs 41 – 55. The complexity is increased in these designs. Some of the elements seem impossible to achieve with the limited stencils available.
Notice designs 53 – 55 each contain <u>two</u> convergences.

Work on the Sheet
Students complete the page.

Closure - Discussion for Insight
Summarize the instrument, the concepts and strategies developed.

www.ingramcontent.com/pod-product-compliance
Lightning Source LLC
Chambersburg PA
CBHW020949230426
43666CB00005B/248